3 arcs
since 2013
LC 2015

D1608782

INSIDE SPECIAL FORCES ™

BLACK OPS
AND OTHER SPECIAL MISSIONS OF THE
U.S. MARINE CORPS SPECIAL OPERATIONS COMMAND

J. Poolos

rosen publishing's
rosen central

New York

Published in 2013 by The Rosen Publishing Group, Inc.
29 East 21st Street, New York, NY 10010

Copyright © 2013 by The Rosen Publishing Group, Inc.

First Edition

Library of Congress Cataloging-in-Publication Data

Poolos, Jamie.
Black ops and other special missions of the U.S. Marine Corps Special Operations Command/J. Poolos.—1st ed.
    p. cm.—(Inside Special Forces)
Includes bibliographical references and index.
ISBN 978-1-4488-8383-7 (library binding)—
ISBN 978-1-4488-8390-5 (pbk.)—
ISBN 978-1-4488-8391-2 (6-pack)
1. United States. Marine Special Operations Command.
2. Special forces (Military science)—United States.
3. Special operations (Military science)—United States.
4. Iraq War, 2003-2011—Commando operations. I. Title.
VE23.P65 2013
359.9'6—dc23

2012018783

Manufactured in the United States of America

CPSIA Compliance Information: Batch #W13YA: For further information, contact Rosen Publishing, New York, New York, at 1-800-237-9932.

CONTENTS

LIKE MOST MILITARY PROGRAMS in the United States, the U.S. Marine Special Forces was created out of a need. Many years ago, U.S. Marine Special Operations were first called upon to fight in Tripoli and the Barbary Coast in Africa. Later, they fought in the Spanish-American War and the Boxer Rebellion. While the army, navy, and air force all have active special forces, it was thought that the highly trained marines satisfied the requirements for special forces personnel. Then the terorist attacks of September 11, 2001, changed everything.

It was that shockingly tragic disaster that motivated the Marine Corps to assess its plans to deal with the world's evolving terrorst threats. As a result, the Marine Corps Special Operations Command (MCSOCOM) Detachment One was created as a pilot program.

The detachment was activated in June 2003 at Camp Pendleton, California, to test and refine the U.S. Marine Special Ops concept in real-world environments. Det 1, as the detachment came to be

A Marine Spec Ops battalion leader is on hyper-alert, his senses fully activated, during a reconnaissance exercise in the southeastern United States.

known, would go on to valiantly demonstrate the merits of dedicated marine special ops in the global war on terrorism and pave the way for MARSOC, the official United States Marine Corps Forces Special Operations Command.

MARSOC is a part of both the U.S. Marine Corps and the U.S. Special Operations Command (SOCOM). Today there are three units. The Marine Special Operations Regiment (MSOR), the Marine Special Operations School, and the Marine Special Operations Intelligence Battalion.

THE MISSIONS OF MARSOC

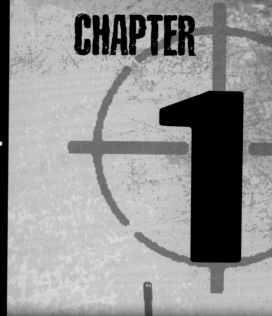

THE MARINE SPECIAL OPERA-TIONS Regiment (MSOR) is the primary combat unit of MARSOC. It maintains four umbrella objectives under which all operations fall. Direct action operations include strikes of short duration and small-scale offensive actions. These are conducted as a special operation in hostile or politically sensitive environments. They employ specialized military capabilities to seize, destroy, capture, or recover designated targets.

The level of physical and political risk is high, and the use of force to achieve objectives is precise. Examples of direct action operations include raids on radar stations, prisoner of war rescue, and the capture of enemy command.

A member of the U.S. Marine Corps Special Operations Command team demonstrates the high altitude–high opening (HAHO) technique during a double-bag static-line parachute course.

Operational techniques associated with direct action objectives include infiltration, attack, and exfiltration. Secrecy is almost always of the utmost importance when it comes to direct action operations, so operational techniques that minimize the chance of detection are used. Infiltration is often done by helicopter using ropes or ladders or by airplane using high altitude–low opening (HALO) or high altitude–high opening (HAHO) jump techniques. Sometimes teams infiltrate by boat.

Forces must avoid detection during the attack phase of an operation so teams use explosives whenever they can to destroy a target. The explosives are set on a delayed fuse, enabling safer exfiltration before the explosion increases the likelihood of detection. This means the members of a direct action unit must be trained in explosives and demolition. Sometimes attacks involve snipers who sneak toward a target undetected before engaging. Once the attack is complete, teams must exfiltrate, or leave, the scene. Again, teams prefer to remain undetected. Often a team exfiltrates using the same means by which it arrived.

Special reconnaissance operations require highly trained teams to operate behind enemy lines or in the enemy's natural habitat, avoiding detection by the enemy, and engaging the enemy with force only as a last resort. Examples of special reconnaissance operations can involve the reconnaissance of potential routes over land and water, directing fire support and precision strikes, the placement and recovery of sensors, and poststrike reconnaissance.

Operational techniques associated with special reconnaissance missions include capturing data via basic photography and drawing, the determination of coordinates using global positioning systems and beacons, and the general and specific assessment of situations and environments. Many teams employ their expertise in thermal imaging and imaging radar. Special reconnaissance teams are often

A marine from the U.S. Marine Corps Special Operations Command observes a fire team conducting counterterrorism operations in the Trans-Saharan region of Africa.

highly trained in gathering information by acoustics and means of electronic warfare.

COUNTERTERRORISM

Counterterrorism operations are focused responses to terrorist threats. The objectives of these operations is to prevent the enemy from using tactics associated with terrorism, whether such prevention is through preparation or direct engagement with the enemy. Examples of counterterrorism operations are hostage rescue, sieges of enemy strongholds or hideouts, patrolling at-risk events, protecting government officials, and reconnaissance.

Operational techniques associated with counterterrorism missions include any reconnaissance techniques and infiltration and exfiltration methods. They also include techniques associated with direct engagement, including preemptive attacks.

FOREIGN INTERNAL DEFENSE

Foreign internal defense operations involve the defense of a host nation from a rebellion, the goal being to prevent or control violence. When fighting is required, the host nation's army or a local police force engages the rebels.

Examples of foreign internal defense operations include the training of host nation commanders in tactical operations tailored to the threat, including on-the-job training during actual missions.

Operational techniques associated with foreign internal defense missions include various methods

MARSOC MISSION STATEMENT

U.S. Marine Corps Forces Special Operations Command (MARSOC), as the U.S Marine Corps component of U.S. Special Operations command (USSOCOM), recruits, trains, organizes, equips, and, when directed by the commander, USSOCOM deploys task-organized, scalable, and responsive U.S. Marine Corps Special Operations Forces (MARSOF) worldwide to accomplish the special operations (SO) mission assigned by the commander of USSOCOM and/or in support of combatant commanders and other agencies.

of needs assessment and corresponding instruction. Subjects can include all aspects of warfare, such as reconnaissance, long- and short-range weapons, field tactics, and communications, to name a few.

INFORMATION OPERATIONS

This class of operation is concerned with information technology as a means to develop an advantage over an enemy through the distribution of propaganda or through the control or sabotage of the technology by which information is delivered. Examples of information operations are the sabotage or hijacking of television and radio transmissions, the destruction of telecommunications networks, and cyberwarfare.

Operational techniques associated with information operations include conventional infiltration, attack, and exfiltration tactics, demolition, and the hacking of computer and satellite networks. They may also involve spreading misinformation through any available means.

UNCONVENTIONAL WARFARE

Unconventional warfare operations, otherwise known as guerrilla warfare, involve a variety of

Muslim guerrilla soldiers of the Moro Islamic Liberation Front patrol Camp Darapanan, their base in southern Maguindanao province in the Philippines.

13

creative or unexpected strategies and actions that attempt to destabilize an enemy.

Examples of unconventional warfare include the harassment of enemy troops and encampments and arming and training resistance fighters.

OTHER OBJECTIVES

The Marine Special Operations School (MSOS) "is the training and educational component in support of MARSOC." It screens and selects marines for missions under the command of MARSOC. Selectees receive entry-level training in the standards, strategies, and techniques of MARSOC. The Marine Special Operations Intelligence Battalion is charged with maintaining combat readiness and generating intelligence for MARSOC personnel engaged in training and operations worldwide.

SELECTION, TRAINING, WEAPONS, AND EQUIPMENT

CHAPTER 2

BEFORE A MARINE CAN BECOME part of the Spec Ops team, he must undergo a rigorous selection process and extensive training. Before he can even begin the training and selection process, he must demonstrate his fitness by hiking uphill for 12 miles (19.3 kilometers) with a 45-pound (20.4 kilogram) pack in three hours and thirty minutes or less and tread water in a swimming pool for half an hour. For the marine, it only gets harder.

APSOC

All candidates participate in a comprehensive screening process. Candidates for Spec Ops are selected based on intellectual aptitude, physical ability, psychological profile, and—most important—interest. All candidates go through the three-week Assessment and Selection Preparatory and Orientation Course (ASPOC) to establish a baseline for training. During this preparatory screening process, marines learn and demonstrate techniques they will use to maintain overall combat fitness throughout the next phase of training and evaluation.

Major General Dennis J. Hejilik, the first to command U.S. Marine Corps Special Forces, summed up the initial screening in an interview with the *Marine Corps Times*: "We put that individual Marine

U.S. Marine Corps Special Operations candidates begin their day with a long, hard run during the Assessment and Selection Preparatory and Orientation Course.

TARGET ACQUISITION SYSTEMS

Sophisticated optics play an important role in special forces. Aiming and illumination systems, holographic weapon sites, and image intensified systems are used to guide ordnance to its target. The EOTech M553 HOLO weapon sight is one such device. It provides an unobscured image of a target in any light condition.

under physical and mental stress. He gets a minimal amount of sleep, and he gets the amount of food and water that he needs to operate effectively under stress. Probably the biggest thing that we've found out is every human being has a natural fear of the unknown."

RIFLES

The rifle is any special force's most personal weapon. A favorite combination for some time has been the M4 carbine or M16 assault rifle with the attached M203 grenade launcher. One of the newest and most versatile weapons is the SCAR, a self-loading automatic sniper and assault rifle. The SCAR was designed with multiple barrels that can be quickly interchanged to accommodate any tactical situation.

SNIPER RIFLES

The ability to take out small targets in close quarters and over long distances is a major tactical

U.S. Marine Corps Special Operations personnel have access to the most cutting-edge weapons and tactical gear, such as the Special Operations Combat Assault Rifle (SCAR).

advantage for Spec Ops shooters. While the Russia made Dragunov was the world's first purpose-built military-precision marksman's rifle, the M40 famil is the most popular sniper rifle among marine special forces. The M82 has an effective range of 1,64 yards (1,500 meters), more than sixteen football fields, and is used to disable armored vehicles.

TACTICAL GEAR

U.S. Marine Special Forces rely on the best equipment available to operate in a number of demanding environments. State-of-the-art radios, headsets, GP devices, antenna, thermal imaging devices, strobes, smoke grenades, as well as the advanced packing systems in which they are carried, help Marine Spe Ops accomplish their full missions.

VEHICLES

Because Marine Special Forces infiltrate and extricate by land, air, and sea, they have used customizec dune buggies, helicopters, and boats. The most useful of all is the HMMWV, reinforced with armor and a machine gun and a missile launcher mounted to its roof. These carry all the equipment the special force need while they are out on mounted patrol. When a boat is necessary to deliver marines to their target, the high-speed, extreme-weather capable rigid inflat able boat (RIB) is called into action.

"TIP OF THE SPEAR"

IN EARLY 2003, the marines of the 1st Reconnaissance Battalion were called into action. While the Pentagon, in its quest to obliterate global terrorism, laid plans to invade Iraq, 1st Recon got ready to pitch in.

At the time, high-level command knew the plan called for these men to be the first to hit the ground when the time came to fight. But 1st Recon knew something different was in the air. For many months, they had been training almost exclusively in field tactics favored by Spec Ops. They had spent a lot of time and effort working in small teams that are quietly inserted by air or boat, then moving toward the target on foot to accomplish a preplanned mission.

Whether the objective was direct action, reconnaissance, or any other objective for which they were purposed, the target was always known at the outset of the operation. In this case, they were told the objective was a bridge that crossed the Euphrates River. Intel showed that in order to move additional forces forward into Iraq, the bridge would have to be captured and controlled. But the Pentagon had other ideas.

The circumstances of the invasion of Iraq required a different approach. This time the 1st Reconnaissance Battalion would deploy as a full battalion, operating large convoys of HMMWVs from

Serving as the "tip of the spear," 155 mm Howitzers line up near the Iraqi border in Kuwait in February 2003, as marines and other friendly forces ready for the invasion of Iraq.

21

the south as it pushed through the wide open desert, across the border and into Iraq. This new strategy was part of the Pentagon Doctrine of Maneuver Warfare, a new approach that was being used for the first time in the invasion of Iraq. It emphasized light forces moving rapidly across the battlefield. The marines would rely on speed rather than stealth or firepower to accomplish their goals. 1st Recon would be, as they call it, the "tip of the spear." As it pushed into Iraq, a large force of American troops would follow.

INTO IRAQ

In March 2003, the marines of 1st Recon set out from Camp Matilda, a base camp in northern Kuwait, and moved along Route 7 toward the Euphrates River. They were joined by Company D, 4th Reconnaissance Battalion, Marine Forces Reserve, who were on the ground to support Operation Iraqi Freedom. 1st Recon and the marines of 4th Recon kept a sharp eye out for Iraqi soldiers as well as terrorists dressed in civilian clothes. Intelligence indicated only light resistance in the area, and on the first day they had little action but the processing of three enemy prisoners of war (EPW). Later, they captured more EPW and uncovered multiple mine fields.

On March 24, as they approached the Euphrates River, the marines engaged the enemy in earnest for the first time as they advanced along the south side of the river until they reached the bridge at An Nasiriyah. They responded with sniper fire, small-arms fire, and machine-gun fire. They then pulled back to regroup for a river crossing. On March 25, the battalion crossed the Euphrates into the city of An Nasiriyah, where they supported operations against Iraqi militia. Instead of securing the bridge and the city, they kept moving, keeping with the Pentagon's agenda of speed as a winning strategy.

LOOKING FOR TROUBLE

The next task was to move across a 115 mile (185 kilometers) stretch of agricultural and urban corridor

Soldiers from the 4th U.S. Marines Regiment are caught in a sandstorm between An Nasiryah and An Najaf, as they fight their way to Baghdad, Iraq.

23

between the cities of An Nasiriyah and Al Kut. This area was stocked with well trained fedayeen guerrilla fighters. During this phase of the mission, 1st Recon was responsible for attracting ambushes. That is, the marines' primary objective was to get the enemy to attack them and in doing so reveal their positions. This tactic is called a screen. Driving seventy open-topped Humvees and trucks with light armor in advance of the seven-thousand-strong Regimental Combat Team One, the battalion would literally run over ambushes so the enemy would have no choice but to engage. In short, they were looking for trouble.

On March 26 the battalion received orders to conduct reconnaissance of Qalat Sikar airfield in support of an attack by a British parachute regiment. Without much time to plan, the marines of 1st Recon relied on their quick-strike training. Because they were so successful at softening up the enemy forces protecting the space, their command directed them to move forward onto the airfield and confront any and all enemies. In the heat of the fight, they learned that the British operation had been scrapped. The battalion was asked to secure and hold the airfield, which it did. The marines remained on premises until March 30, when they moved out to penetrate deeper into Iraq.

CLEARING A PATH

Over the next few weeks, the battalion continued its reconnaissance, screening the territory between An Nasiriyah and Al Kut. Its convoy of Humvees and

A SOCOM COMMANDER'S PRIORITIES

1. Deter, Disrupt and Defeat Terrorist Threats

2. Develop and Support Our People and Families

3. Sustain and Modernize the Force

4. Plan and Conduct Special Operations

5. Focus on Quality

6. Equip the Operator

7. Emphasize Persistent, Culturally Attuned Engagement

8. Care for Our People and Families

9. Upgrade SOF Mobility

10. Foster Interagency Cooperation

11. Train and Educate the Joint Warrior/Diplomat

12. Obtain Persistent Intelligence, Surveillance, and Reconnaissance Systems

—From the United States Special Operations Command

light trucks patrolled Route 7 as the marines made their way north.

The armor attachment advanced to quash the enemy positions, eliminating a squad of enemy soldiers by machine-gun fire from 164 feet (50 meters).

As additional enemy forces flanked the marines, the radioman called in close air support. The airstrikes were effective, eliminating enemy threats. By now the bridge was nearly destroyed, so another route was scouted. The battalion moved about 9.3 miles (15 km) to the south of Al Muf, where the marines crossed the river safely and continued their mission of reconnaissance and support.

There were many other encounters during this operation. The marines of 1st Recon undertook such tasks as setting up roadblocks, finding mine fields, and processing natives who fled from conflicts to the north. They captured a wide variety of weapons and destroyed a number of weapon caches that included small firearms, mortars, and RPGs. They operated as a complete battalion or as coordinated companies, as when Alpha Company separated from the battalion and assisted in the liberation of the town of Ash Shatrah. At Al Haay, 1st Recon surrounded the city, setting up roadblocks that shut off escape routes. Meanwhile, the Regimental Combat Team 1 captured the town. In a daring night mission, the marines of 1st Recon seized the bridge into Al Muwaffaqiyah. They continued to move north, paving the way for the substantial number of American forces that followed.

INTO AL KUT

Finally the marines of 1st Recon neared the city of Al Kut, at the northern end of their reconnaissance area. As the marines moved north toward their objective, orders came to stop the advance and leave Al Kut untouched. Unbeknown to them, they were actually acting as decoys as part of a larger plan designed to lead the Iraqi command to believe the U.S. forces would come through Al Kut. But at the last minute, the large number of American troops advancing behind 1st Recon were ordered to move toward Baghdad by another route. By then, the Iraqi forces, believing the U.S. forces came in the wake of 1st Recon, had already massed their firepower at Al Kut, with no one to fight.

U.S. Marines clear a building in Al Kut, Iraq, in the early days of Operation Iraqi Freedom. First Recon played a key role in making cities like Al Kut safer for American troops.

The seven thousand U.S. forces that followed 1st Recon reached Baghdad, the capital of Iraq, unscathed. When they arrived, they were fresh and ready to fight. 1st Recon had done its job in clearing the way. But the work was not done. As the battle for Baghdad raged, the marines of 1st Recon circled north toward Baqubah to perform reconnaissance and to engage the Republican Guard units—Iraq's elite fighting forces— that were believed to be in the area. They were joined by the Light Armored 1st Marine Division's 1st Light Armored Reconnaissance Battalion (LAR) and a company of reservist reconnaissance marines. They engaged the Republican Guard, which attempted to resist the marines' advance toward Baqubah, in a number of battles. While Companies A, B and D and the LAR company took positions that would block an advance of Iraqi forces, Company C conducted a reconnaissance of the Iraqi 41st Armored Brigade and Al Nida Republican Guard headquarters.

Over the course of about two months, the U.S. Marine Special Forces of the 1st Reconnaissance Battalion had accomplished its mission with flying colors. The marines had functioned as the "tip of the spear," safely leading large numbers of critical U.S. forces into the capital of Iraq, where they could conduct their operations without the fear of large-scale enemy attacks. The battalion remained on the line until it redeployed from Kuwait to California on June 3, 2003.

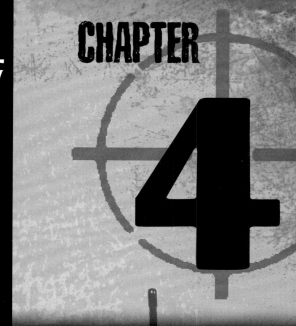

THE TAKING OF AN NAJAF

I **N OCTOBER 2002**, Commandant James Logan Jones, the highest ranking officer of the United States Marine Corps, ordered the creation of a permanent United States Special Operations Command (USSOCOM) employment. On June 20, 2003, a special detachment of 102 marines was activated as a proof of concept for this employment. These marines were Detachment One.

In April 2004, after intense training and the completion of U.S. Navy Special Warfare Certification, Detachment One, or Det 1, arrived in Iraq, where they were scheduled to complete a six-month deployment in support of Operation Iraqi Freedom. In this pilot program, Det 1 would operate under Naval Special Warfare Group One, working hand in

hand with U.S. Navy Spec Ops, and attempt to prove
that the marines belonged in U.S. Special Operations
Command. During its deployment, Det 1 participated
in a wide variety of operations, including reconnaissance, direct actions, raids, snatches, and demolitions, to name a few. But one of the most notable and
heroic was the taking of An Najaf.

By this stage of the war, An Najaf had developed
a reputation as a tough town with a lot of action.
One hundred miles (160 km) due south of Baghdad,
An Najaf was of great strategic importance for

*U.S. Marines from the 11th Expeditionary Unit patrol the busy
streets of An Najaf in southern Iraq on September 11, 2004.*

one reason: it was the home of Imam Ali Mosque and thus holy ground for all Shia Muslims. In April 2004 the Shia had attacked coalition forces but had been defeated. When the coalition forces, mostly U.S. Army units, turned back the attackers, they handed control of An Najaf over to the 11th Marine Expeditionary Unit. But over the next few months the enemy lay in wait, planning their next attack. By August, large numbers of Shia militiamen were ready to attack on the orders of Muqtada al-Sadr, one of Iraq's most influential religious and political leaders. When that order came, the militiamen came out of hiding and made their presence known.

TASK UNIT RAIDER

Undermanned, the 11th Marine Expeditionary Unit held its positions and called in reinforcements for what would turn out to be a full-on fight. In response, the Combined Joint Special Operations Task Force-Arabian Peninsula ordered a contingent under the 1st Battalion, 5th Special Forces Group to provide support in An Najaf. Det 1, which at the time had the nickname Task Unit Raider, was instructed to provide sniper support.

On August 17, 2004, Det 1's subdetachment joined a U.S. Army Special Forces convoy and headed to An Najaf. The team was led by Master Sergeant Terry M. Wyrick. It included seven snipers under Gunnery Sergeant John A. Dailey, one air support specialist, and one corpsman. Just prior to its departure, the

DET 1'S SNIPER WEAPONS IN AN NAJAF

The .50-caliber Barrett is designed for long-range targets. It was too big to be used much in the close confines of An Najaf, but it is powerful enough to blow large holes in walls. The Barrett is the only semiautomatic .50-caliber rifle available. It is 57 inches (145 centimeters) in length and weighs almost 40 pounds (18 kg). The magazine holds ten rounds. A muzzle brake at the end of the barrel reduces kick, making the Barrett a comfortable large-caliber weapon. It has an effective range of more than 1,500 yards (1,372 m) and can shoot to distances greater than 1.5 miles (2.4 km).

The Barrett .50 caliber is one of the most powerful and stealthy weapons in the sniper's arsenal, giving the marine a clear advantage over the enemy.

The 7.62mm SR-25 is a semiautomatic sniper rifle with great range and accuracy. The gun is built by the Knight's Armament Company, based in Florida. The U.S. Marine Spec Ops soldiers use it with multiple optics and sound suppression devices. In a properly constructed sniper hide, a marine with a suppressed SR-25 could engage multiple targets in quick succession without ever giving away the position. The rifle is 45.4 inches (115 cm) long and weighs 15.3 pounds (6.9 kg). The magazine holds twenty rounds.

team secured sniper weapons from another team that had just returned from a fierce battle in the city of Al Kut. Det 1 was joined by the 2nd Battalion of the 7th U.S. Calvary, which would provide support and reinforcements in An Najaf. Command wanted plenty of numbers to combat the many Shia militiamen. Det 1's mission was to deploy snipers to support a ground attack on the mosque.

ASSESSING AND ENGAGING

The journey to An Najaf was eye-opening to many of the Det 1 marines. Once in position, the marines observed the situation without engaging the enemy, even though the enemy directed small-arms fire their way. They took note of the terrain, special features like walls and buildings that could offer shelter to militiamen in flight, and enemy locations.

A marine from the 11th Expeditionary Unit listens for instructions as a convoy enters the city of An Najaf, Iraq. Communications are always a vital part of the U.S. Marine Special Ops.

They spent the entire first day in An Najaf performing reconnaissance on the mosque and surrounding areas, moving from location to location in order to get a complete picture of the battlefield. They recorded their observations and took them back to headquarters to share with their command.

In fact, the snipers were so effective and the enemy was so devastated that a cease-fire was called. By all appearances, the enemy had seen enough. The marines of Det 1 withdrew from their outpost and settled in at the Task Force Cougar command post. Anticipating more action later, they refit their gear and awaited further orders. Meanwhile, they received reinforcements in the form of a fires expert and a radioman, both of whom would coordinate radio traffic and enable better communication among the snipers.

The cease-fire collapsed abruptly August 22. The snipers immediately left the command post and moved forward to a new position where they could engage the enemy. On August 23, they moved even closer to the mosque. That day, three marines were injured. The hospital corpsman treated them and arranged for their safe evacuation. The marines retaliated by destroying an enemy mortar position that resulted in four kills.

It wasn't easy for the snipers to identify their targets. Most of the enemy militia were men of all ages, wearing black clothing and green headbands. They often used women and children to screen their movements, believing U.S. soldiers wouldn't risk killing or wounding a civilian in order to kill a fighter. They didn't count on the snipers' advanced training and weapons and Det 1's willingness to use their expertise.

SUPERIOR STRATEGIES

By August 24, the marines of Det 1 had been in An Najaf for nearly a full week. Reinforcements were called in just as the fighting grew more intense. The marines kept the pressure on. They identified probable locations of arms caches and shot and killed any males of "military age" who went in or came out. They called in air support from the army, air force, and marines, depending on which was on duty. They had fresh snipers on weapons twenty-four hours a day in the hot conditions, which made staring into their rifles' optics tiring.

Their strategies were so effective that the ground assault on the mosque never happened. On the night of August 27, Det 1 marines who were close to the mosque witnessed large numbers of Shia gunmen move into the open with their guns. They were surrendering. In the early hours of the following morning, a truce was reached. This time, the cease-fire lasted. Negotiations resulted in al-Sadr and his forces withdrawing from the city. Finally, the authority of the interim Iraqi government had been restored in An Najaf. On August 27, Det 1 marines pulled back to the calvary battalion post. Several days later they travelled back to Baghdad by helicopter and Humvee.

The Det 1 marines had demonstrated the benefits of their skills and training with great success. Along with Task Force Cougar and the 2nd Battalion, 7th Calvary, they played a big part in a major coalition victory. In his history of Det 1, Charles P. Neimeyer, director of Marine Corps history, wrote, "The actions of the Det 1 Marine during the battle of Najaf have no parallel in any other battle of Operation Iraqi Freedom. In a situation that called for a special operations force to completely integrate with a conventional unit as a supporting effort, Task Unit Raider's Marines shone brilliantly."

OPERATION RED THUNDER

IN THE LATE SUMMER OF 2009, Taliban forces still had firm roots in strategic locations throughout Afghanistan. It was the mission of coalition forces to wipe them out. One such location was the city of Shewan. Located in the Farah province, Shewan had been the site of many fierce battles over the years. When the former Soviet Union had invaded Afghanistan during its nine-year war (1979–1988), its forces had tried to capture Shewan and the area around it on several occasions without success. The locals were tough and resilient, and they knew the layout of the terrain very well. Many were farmers, growing poppies that would be sold in the opium trade. Anyone who tried to take the land belonging to these people would have to be ready to fight.

Over the previous few years, the coalition forces had taken the fight to the Taliban, driving them away from Shewan. Believing the enemy had retreated for good, coalition forces would move on to the next battle. When they left, the Taliban would move back in.

Such was the case after a well-known battle between elements from several marine battalions and Taliban insurgents in early August 2008. At that time, combined forces that included Golf Company, 2nd Platoon, 2nd Battalion 7th Marines, and part of the 1st Reconnaissance Battalion were ambushed by

Special Forces and U.S. Army personnel patrol the Taliban stronghold of Shewan in Farah province, Afghanistan.

a large number of Taliban resistance fighters. The marines were outnumbered eight to one against the well-armed Taliban, who were equipped with mortars and rocket-propelled grenades, as well as rifles. It was a hard battle. Even though the marines called in air strikes and F-18s dropped bombs and strafed the city with cannons, the Taliban held on. Late in the night, vehicles carrying approximately one hundred Taliban reinforcements drove into the city. After fifteen hours of heavy combat, the marines prevailed, killing 150 enemy fighters. The majority of the Taliban fighters fled to the mountains to hide.

But following that battle, when the marines pulled out, the Taliban fighters came out of hiding and trickled into the city to assume control once again. Despite the marines' superior fighting, they were not changing much in Shewan. The city's residents, who had hoped the coalition forces would drive out the Taliban and restore normalcy to their lives, had little to be happy about. They were essentially cut off from the outside world and were unable to take full advantage of a medical outreach program the coalition had implemented to help those in need. Because the Taliban controlled the city and the roads leading into it, they controlled the supplies.

When aid in the form of food, medical supplies, and other necessities was delivered to the city, the Taliban fighters would seize it and use it for their own benefit or sell it to residents at high prices. They ran the town, preventing the residents from going about their business safely. They had seized the local mosque as their headquarters, so the elders and residents had no central place to pray. By all measures, the Taliban resistance in Shewan was tough, well equipped, and stubborn. Intelligence indicated more than four hundred fighters were deeply rooted in the city. They would not be driven away easily. Complicating the matter was the fact that General Stanley McChrystal, the commander of the U.S. forces in Afghanistan, wanted to visit the city to assess the progress of the coalition. It became a high priority to drive the Taliban out of Shewan, and not just anyone could do the job. This mission would require soldiers with extensive training and skills.

TAKING SHEWAN

In August 2009, the 1st Marine Special Operations Battalion (MSOB) landed in Afghanistan to join other elements of the Marine Operations Special Command (MARSOC) in a mission to take Shewan from the Taliban. The mission was named Operation Red Thunder. It involved a mix of forces, including 125 Spec Ops marines from MARSOC, more than six hundred Afghan soldiers, and additional Afghan commandos. Additional support would be provided by the 82nd Airborne Division as well as the Afghan National Police. After extensive planning, reconnaissance, and coordination of the various outfits, the operation was set to go.

On September 26, 2009, the operation began with a ground assault on Shewan in which the U.S. Marine

WEAPONS OF THE FUTURE

After the September 11, 2001, terrorist attacks, the U.S. Congress approved a military budget of almost $1.3 trillion to support Operation Iraqi Freedom in Iraq, Operation Enduring Freedom in Afghanistan, and other conflicts. More than $2 billion has been spent on military construction and research. Two important areas are directed energy and exoskeletons.

An example of a directed energy weapon is the active denial system under development at Raytheon, a well-known weapons manufacturer. This system is a nonlethal crowd control device that directs a focused beam of wave energy, which heats

The HULC exoskeleton enables soldiers to repetitively lift and carry heavy loads all day long, giving soldiers a critical advantage over the enemy.

up the water in the outer layers of a person's skin. It creates a burning sensation, like a sunburn. Test have shown that the system is effective in controlling people.

Several defense contractors are well along in the development of hydraulic-powered exoskeletons that soldiers wear on their legs or arms and are powered by batteries or by vehicles connected by cable. The exoskeletons enable soldiers to lift and carry up to 50 pounds (23 kg) in each arm or 198 pounds (90 kg) over long distances with almost no effort.

Special Forces and the Afghan soldiers fired into the city. They were supported from the air by numerous types of airplanes and helicopters, including AFSOC AC-130 gunships, U.S. Army AH-64 Apaches, U.S. Marine AH-1 Cobras, U.S. Air Force A-10 Thunderbolts, and F-16 Falcon fighters. The coalition had brought its big guns to the fight.

Immediately the fighting was heavy as both sides poured round after round on the other. Heavy Taliban fire kept the coalition forces pinned down, and marine and Afghan ground forces found it difficult to advance their positions. During the first day of fighting, the AC-130 gunships exhausted all of their ammunition. But they had done their job, causing untold destruction on Taliban strongholds and making it impossible for the enemy to move around within Shewan. Over the battle's four grueling days, the precision fire of these powerful gunships was the most important tactical advantage the marines and Afghan soldiers had in their assault. As fire from the AC-130s and other aircraft ripped into the Taliban, the 1st Marine Special Operations Battalion was able to lead the Afghan military in a slow, methodical advance on the city.

Inch by inch the marines crawled forward. As they reached advantageous positions, they scoped the targets with advanced optical equipment like the SU-231/PEQ, which displays holographic images of a target, or the AN/PAS-13, which is capable of detecting targets in total darkness. The marines who perform fire control view the targets, observe where the fire is actually striking, and shout instructions to the marines manning the weapons in order to guide the fire to the target. The accurate fire eliminated the vicious Taliban fighters or drove them from their well-defended positions.

By the time they entered the city, the enemy was on the defensive. Many Taliban had fled or were looking for the opportunity to leave Shewan before the marines could capture them. Operating in small teams, the 1st MSOB led the Afghan soldiers as they went house to house, kicking in doors, chasing out Taliban, and securing areas of the city. Eventually, they cleared Shewan of Taliban insurgents, and the residents were free to move about. The friendly forces took stock of their casualties. In four days of fighting, one marine had been killed. Three Afghan soldiers had been killed. They reported no civilian deaths. Most important, sixty-five Taliban fighters had been killed.

REBUILDING SHEWAN

By running the Taliban out of Shewan, the U.S. Marine Special Forces and their Afghan army train-ees had made it possible for supplies to reach the city's citizens. Coalition forces and other groups from the international community would now be able to safely deliver much needed medical sup-plies, food, and other important things. The resi-dents of Shewan again had the promise of returning

An officer works with village elders during the rebuilding phase of Shewan village in Farah province, Afghanistan. Human relations are an important part of Special Operations.

to life as usual. The shura, or village elders, could enter the white mosque the Taliban had been using as a headquarters. They could worship and lead the town as they had before the Taliban had disrupted their lives.

But the work of the 1st MSOB wasn't finished. If the marines left the city, the Taliban insurgents would simply return and take over the city again. They had to strengthen Shewan so the Taliban could not intimidate the city again. Plans were made to rebuild Shewan and keep the Taliban out. The 1st MSOB and the Afghan soldiers remained in Shewan to teach the residents how they could live free of Taliban rule. They showed them that Shewan could once again be a safe, prosperous place to live. One of the biggest hurdles was to demonstrate to the residents that money could flow again now that the Taliban wasn't in control of the local economy. The marines also worked with the leaders of the village to plan the rebuilding of physical structures, such as new schools. They awarded contracts to Afghans to accomplish this, funding construction and creating jobs. Roads were repaired. Damaged buildings were fixed. In addition, they taught the poppy farmers to grow other crops that they could sell locally.

When General Stanley McChrystal visited Shewan in January 2010, he said, "The last time I was here [in Farah province], I heard firsthand about how bad Shewan was getting. This time I got to actually go there and see the recent progress for myself, thanks to the noteworthy clearing operation there. Your Marines have done some amazing work here, and the people of Afghanistan will not forget it. The American people are proud of you."

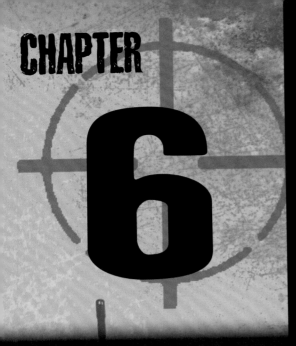

CHAPTER 6

PIRATES ON THE MAGELLAN STAR

WHILE U.S. MARINE SPEC OPS is best known for its role in unconventional warfare operations in the Middle East, it is also called upon to act outside of the typical theaters of war. Operations can include anything from reconnaissance of suspected terrorist or extremist threats to suppression of airplane hijackers to actual rescues. One such operation involved a branch of the U.S. Marine Special Operations called the marine expeditionary unit. These marines are not part of the MARSOC command structure, yet their purpose shares much in common.

A marine expeditionary unit (MEU) is a quick reaction force that is deployed and ready for immediate response to any crisis worldwide. Each MEU includes elements that allow it to operate with a number of strengths. These include a ground combat element and an aviation combat element. The ground combat element is a reinforced infantry battalion. The aviation combat element combines a helicopter squadron, a logistics combat element (which supplies equipment), and a command element (which provides intelligence and direction).

These elements operate as a single force under one command, a strategy that increases their speed and reaction time. Each unit has its own tanks, Humvees, helicopters, bulldozer, weapons, and a wide variety of additional gear. An MEU has all of its personnel and equipment staged, or ready to use, at all times. Unlike other Special Operations units, it brings everything it needs when it goes into action. Its main objective is to get to the target fast. Additional supplies and support units can catch up later.

There are MEUs deployed to areas of operations around the world. The 11th, 13th, and 15th MEUs, stationed at Camp Pendleton, California, operate in the Pacific and Indian oceans, including the Persian Gulf. The 22nd, 24th, and 26th MEUs are stationed at Marine Corps Base Camp Lejeune, North Carolina, and operate in the Atlantic Ocean and in the Mediterranean Sea. The 31st MEU is the only permanently forward-deployed MEU, based at Marine Corps Base Camp Smedley D. Butler, in Okinawa, Japan. It operates in the Pacific Ocean. These units are ready to roll on short notice. Such was the case in 2008, when an unexpected call came in over the radio.

TWO ACTS OF PIRACY

The USS *Dubuque*, an Austin-class amphibious dock ship, was operating approximately 1,500 miles (2,414 km) from its command ship, the USS *Peleliu*. These boats were attached to Combined Task Force 151 (CTF-151), the international counterpiracy task force. The *Dubuque* had spent the night of September 9, 2011, escorting vessels through shipping corridors in the Internationally Recommended Transit Corridor in the Gulf of Aden, off the coast of Yemen. The Turkish frigate TCG *Gökçeada*, a CTF-151 flagship, received distress calls from the *Olib G*, a Greek-owned chemical tanker flying the Maltese flag. The *Olib G* was in trouble. The *Gökçeada* sprung into action, launching its helicopters. When they flew into range, the helicopter crews reported seeing pirates on board with rocket propelled grenades, so they kept their distance.

Just then, another call came in. In an unrelated incident, the *Magellan Star* had reported being boarded by pirates. The *Magellan Star* was a German-owned cargo ship that flew the Antiguan flag. At the time, it was traveling from Vietnam to Spain. The *Gökçeada* abruptly moved to the area where the *Magellan Star* was operating, where its crew found an unmanned skiff the pirates had used for transport.

Meanwhile, the *Dubuque*, nearly 15 nautical miles (27.8 km) away, sped to the *Magellan Star* to lend a hand. It was equipped with all the necessary personnel and gear to take down the pirates. On board was Captain Alexander Martin, the 15th MEU's maritime raid force commander. More than anyone, he was aware of how well-prepared his platoon was for this action. They had been rehearsing for such a situation for the past year. Once they got the word to stand by, the 15th MEU swung into action.

They knew exactly what to do. They grabbed body armor, weapons, ammunition, and communications and breaching gear and assembled it all in a common area. Every piece of gear was checked to make sure it functioned properly before a detailed inspection by assistant team leaders. Some of the other important equipment included flotation devices, chemical lights, breathing devices, medical equipment, and night vision equipment. Once everything checked out, the overall mission commander, Lieutenant Colonel Joseph Clearfield, gave the order for sixty-minute ready posture, which meant the platoon could be ready for action in an hour.

As the 15th MEU readied, more details about the crisis trickled in. The crew of the *Magellan Star* had locked itself in the engine room and was not in direct danger of being taken hostage. They had also disabled the engine, leaving the *Magellan Star* dead in the water, with no way to move. In fact, when the pirates learned the engines would not start, they made a call to the ship's owners in Dortmund, Germany, and demanded to know where the crew was. They also wanted to know how to start the ship's

LIGHT ASSAULT BOATS

U.S. Marine Spec Ops operating at sea or coastal areas rely on the rigid hull inflatable boat (RHIB) for insertion and extraction and patrol and coastal surveillance. The boat's construction makes it perfect for high speed and a low rate of detection. Its hull is made of tough reinforced plastic so it can withstand collisions with rocks and rough beaches. It is kept afloat with inflatable gunwales made from strong fabric. The 35-foot (10.7 m) RHIB is powered by two large turbo-charged diesel Caterpillar motors that connect to a jet pump. It has saddle seats for eight marines and a crew of three. It can attain speeds of more than 45 knots (83.3 kilometers per hour) and has a maximum range of 190 nautical miles (352 km) in rough seas with high winds.

The boat carries a wealth of equipment, including radar and GPS, an identification transponder to determine if nearby craft are friends or foes, and satellite communications, as well as weapons such as the M2HB .50-caliber machine gun, the M240 belt-fed machine gun, and the MK19 40mm grenade launcher. It is highly transportable and can even be parachuted into water from a C-130 cargo plane or from a helicopter.

engines. With some sense of humor, the owners told the pirates the crew was on holiday and that the engines had been having trouble. Realizing they'd never get the information they wanted, the angry pirates hung up.

But the pirates remained defiant and aggressive. They were pointing their weapons at the warships and making demands. They had refused to surrender. By the time this information came in, all of the Huey aircraft and Cobra gunships had been prepped and were ready to go should they be needed. Captain Martin and his men went over the "template," or plan, and handed out assignments to various individuals. But the platoon was held back while decisions about the appropriate action were pushed up the chain of command. It was late at night before they were made aware that the president of the United States was considering the problem and that they had the go-ahead to attack at dawn.

TAKING BACK THE *MAGELLAN STAR*

Just before the sun rose the following morning, twenty-four soldiers of the 15th MEU set off in fast-moving inflatable craft and moved as rapidly as they could to the assault point. In addition to the *Dubuque*, the warship USS *Princeton* and the *Gökçeada* had surrounded the *Magellan Star*. Helicopters hovered in the area with gunmen aboard ready to fire on any pirates who raised a weapon to the assault team.

When the platoon boarded the *Magellan Star.*, they swarmed the deck and quickly took up offensive positions before moving forward. In such close quarters, they had to be extremely careful not to fire upon one another by mistake. The pirates' reaction to such force was predictable. Some surrendered, and some fled, but none fired back. The platoon captured the nine pirates, who turned out to be Somalian, without firing a single shot. "I've never been more proud than I was watching the balance of violence of action and professional restraint that is the hallmark of a

Special Forces from the U.S. Navy and the U.S. Marine Corps speed toward the Magellan Star *after pirates seized the ship in the Gulf of Aden.*

true professional warrior," said Captain Martin in his blog on the United States Naval Institute's Web site. But the job wasn't done yet. They still had to rescue the crew.

In order to escape the pirates, the crew had barricaded themselves in quarters behind a large steel door. As the hours passed, they moved deeper and deeper into the ship's interior, locking the big doors as they retreated. Finally, they reached the engine room, which was as far as they could go.

Now, between the crew and the marines were a number of locked steel doors. Because the crew had no battery power in the emergency phone they carried, they could not hear the marines and were unaware that the pirates had been captured. Frightened and uncertain, they would not open the doors. So the marines got out their thermal torches and power saws and began cutting into the ship's thick steel. They took turns operating the cutting equipment and standing guard.

Three hours later, the marines reached the engine room. They broadcast a message through a bullhorn indicating they had taken the ship and that the pirates had been captured. Still, the crew, mostly Filipinos, Ukranians, and Poles, would not come out. One of the marines, Sergeant Max Chesmore, ripped an American flag patch from his uniform and showed it to the captain. That was all the captain needed to see. He led the relieved crew out of the engine room. Finally, the crew was secure.

Thorough training and advanced preparedness had enabled the 15th MEU to conduct an advanced military operation successfully and without a casualty. But they weren't alone. It was an integrated effort that demonstrated the importance of planning and repetition in rehearsal of the MEU's most important skills: speed, surprise, and purpose in execution. Lieutenant Colonel Clearfield was quoted in a *Washington Post* article about the operation. He said, "It was a combination of speed and overwhelming force. At that point, I think they [the pirates] realized that resistance was futile." The operation also reflected the ability of a coordinated marine and navy effort. Given the combined intelligence and skill of these specialized branches of the United States military, ships passing through this region can feel more safe and secure.

GLOSSARY

AMPHIBIOUS ASSAULT An operation that involves establishing a force on a hostile or potentially hostile shore.

AREA OF OPERATIONS An area where commanders accomplish their missions and protect their forces.

ARMS CACHE A hiding place for weapons.

BATTALION A ground force unit composed of a command and two or more companies.

COMPANY A number of individuals organized as a unit.

CYBERWARFARE The use of computers to attack an enemy's information systems.

DEFIANT To be resistant or to challenge an opposing force.

DEMOLITIONS The act of demolishing or destroying an enemy target, often with explosives.

DEPLOYMENT Strategic movement into a position ready for use.

DIRECT ACTION An action designed to achieve immediate results.

EXOSKELETON A hard external or outside covering.

EXTRICATE To free or release; to liberate.

GUERRILLA A member of an armed force that combats stronger regular forces, like an army or the police.

HOLOGRAPHIC Appearing as a three-dimensional likeness of a thing.

HYDRAULIC To be operated using water or other liquids through a narrow passage, like pipes, hoses, or tubes.

INSURGENT A person who rises up against a strong authority or government.

MILITIAMAN A person enrolled in a military force that is called to drill but serves full-time only in emergencies.

MOSQUE A Muslim temple or place of public worship.

PENTAGON The headquarters of the U.S. Department of Defense.

RECONNAISSANCE A search made for useful information by examining the terrain and environment.

SCREEN A tactic by which a number of marines move to clear an area in advance of a force or asset that follows.

SHIA The plural of Shiite, a member of one of the two main religious divisions of Islam.

STAGED Set up and ready to be used, such as equipment and gear.

TALIBAN A Muslim fundamentalist group.

TERRORISM The use of violence or threats to intimidate for political reasons.

FOR MORE INFORMATION

Canadian Special Operations Regiment (CSOR)
P.O. Box 9999 STN MAIN
Petawawa, ON K8H 2X3
Canada
(800) 467-9877
Web site: http://www.csor-rosc.forces.gc.ca
> The CSOR Web site has information on history, ethics, recruitment, family life, and other aspects of CSOR.

Department of National Defence
Assistant Deputy Minister (Public Affairs)
National Defence Headquarters
Major-General George R. Pearkes Building
101 Colonel By Drive
Ottawa, ON K1A 0K2
Canada
(800) 467-9877
Web site: http://www.cansofcom.forces.gc.ca
> The Department of National Defence has complete information on the Canadian Special Forces, including background information on the units, missions, and contact information.

MARSOC Foundation
P.O. Box 2018
Temecula, CA 92593-2018
(800) 985-0429

Web site: http://www.marsocfoundation.org
This foundation was created to provide support to active duty and medically retired MARSOC personnel and their families.

United States Marine Corps.
New York Public Affairs Office
New York, NY 10022-7513
(212) 784-0160
Web site: http://www.marines.com
This is the most comprehensive resource for the United States Marine Corps. This site has information about the marines' global impact, weapons and equipment, and history. It also has information about what it's like to be a marine and how to become one.

WEB SITES

Due to the changing nature of Internet links, Rosen Publishing has developed an online list of Web sites related to the subject of this book. This site is updated regularly. Please use this link to access the list:

http://www.rosenlinks.com/ISF/SPOP

FOR FURTHER READING

Bradley, Rusty. *Lions of Kandahar: The Story of a Fight Against All Odds*. New York, NY: Bantam Books, 2011.

Flick, Nathanial C. *One Bullet Away: The Making of a Marine Officer*. New York, NY: Houghton Mifflin Company, 2006.

Frederick, Jim. *Time Special Ops: The Hidden War of America's Toughest Warriors*. New York, NY: Time, 2011.

Frederickson, John C. *Fighting Elites: A History of U.S. Special Forces*. Santa Barbara, CA: ABC-CLIO, 2012.

Hearn, Chester G. *Marines: An Illustrated History*. St. Paul, MN: Zenith Press, 2007.

North, Oliver. *American Heroes: In Special Operations*. Nashville, TN: Fidelis Books, 2010.

North, Oliver, and Chuck Holton. *American Heroes: In the Fight Against Radical Islam*. Nashville, TN: Fidelis Books, 2009.

Smith, Michael. *Killer Elite: The Inside Story of America's Most Secret Special Operations Team*. New York, NY: St. Martin's Press, 2008.

Urban, Mark. *Task Force Black: The Explosive True Story of the Secret Special Forces War in Iraq*. New York, NY: St. Martin's Press, 2010.

Wright, Evan. *Generation Kill: Devil Dogs, Iceman, Captain America, and the New Face of American War*. New York, NY: Penguin Group, 2008.

BIBLIOGRAPHY

Barrett.net. "Model 82A1." Retrieved April 3, 2012 (http://barrett.net/firearms/model82a1).

Bauer, Shane. "Iraq's New Death Squad." TheNation .com. Retrieved February 2, 2012 (http://www.the nation.com/article/iraqs-new-death-squad).

Defense Video and Imagery Distribution System. "Joint Force Clears Insurgents in Shewan; Afghan-International Force Interdicts Uzbek Militant in Takhar." Retrieved January 23, 2012 (http://www.dvidshub.net).

Gilman, B. L. "First Reconnaissance Battalion Narrative Summary Re: Operation Iraqi Freedom From 1 Feb to 24 May." 1streconbnassociation.org. Retrieved January 12, 2012 (http://www.1streconbnassociation .org/IFreedom/Bn.htm).

Greenemeier, Larry. "Post-9/11 Technology Brings Exoskeletons, Laser Cannons to 21st Century U.S. Military." *Scientific American*, September 6, 2011. Retrieved April 3, 2012 (http://www.scientific american.com).

Kovach, Gretel C. "Marine Forces in Demand: Special Operations Grows Into Afghan Role." U-T San Diego .com. Retrieved February 21, 2012 (http://www .utsandiego.com).

Kovach, Gretel C. "A New Breed: Marine Special Operations." U-T San Diego.com. Retrieved January 15, 2012 (http://www.utsandiego.com).

Marines.mil. "Heritage." Retrieved January 10, 2012 (http://www.marines.mil/unit/marsoc/Pages/default.aspx).

Piedmont, Lieutenant Colonel John P. Det 1 U.S. Marine Corps. *U.S. Special Operations Command Detachment, 2003-2006: U.S. Marines in the Global War on Terror.* Washington, DC: History Division United States Marine Corps, 2010.

Pushies, Fred. *MARSOC: U.S. Marine Corps Special Operations Command.* Minneapolis, MN: Zenith Press, 2011.

Shadowspear.com. "Machine Guns." Retrieved January 10, 2012 (http://www.shadowspear.com/machineguns/index.1.html).

Shadowspear.com. "Marine Corps Special Operations Command." Retrieved January 10, 2012 (http://www.shadowspear.com).

Shadowspear.com. "Marine Corps Special Operations Forces." Retrieved January 10, 2012 (http://www.shadowspear.com).

Shadowspear.com. "Rifles." Retrieved January 10, 2012 (http://www.shadowspear.com/rifles/index.1.html).

Shadowspear.com. "Sniper Rifles." Retrieved January 10, 2012 (http://www.shadowspear.com/sniper-rifles/index.1.html).

Shadowspear.com. "Special Operations Library." Retrieved January 10, 2012 (http://www.shadowspear.com/special-operations-research.html).

Talton, Trista. "MARSOC: A Work in Progress." Navy Times. Retrieved January 23, 2012 (http://www.navytimes.com/news/2007/09/marine_hejlik_marsoc_070901/).

Wright, Evan. *Generation Kill: Devil Dogs, Iceman, Captain America, and the New Face of American War.* New York, NY: Penguin Group, 2008.

INDEX

ABOUT THE AUTHOR

J. Poolos has written books for young adults on a variety of subjects, including the United States Army Rangers and hostage negotiation. He has written histories and strategy guides for the computer game industry on submarine warfare and on the U.S. Navy SEALs, where he had the privilege of interviewing some of the country's first SEALs.

PHOTO CREDITS

Cover insets U.S. Marine Corps Pictures from left Cpl. Kyle McNally, Cpl. Kyle McNally, Lance Cpl. David J.Adams, Sgt. Pete Thibodeau, 2nd Lt. Jeanscott Dodd, Cpl. Reece Lodder; cover (flare) © iStockphoto.com/Evgeny Terentev; cover (smoke) © iStockphoto.com/Antagain; cover, interior (crosshairs) © iStockphoto.com/marlanu; pp. 4–5, 16, 18 U.S. Marine Corps Forces Special Operations Command; p. 8 Cpl. Kyle McNally, U.S. Marine Corps Pictures; p. 10 Max Blumenfeld, U.S. Marine Corps Pictures; p. 13 Mark Navales/AFP/Getty Images; p. 21 Joe Raedle/Getty Images; p. 23 Laurent Van Der Stockt/Gamma-Rapho/Getty Images; p. 27 Oleg Nikishin/Getty Images; pp. 30, 34 Getty Images; p. 32 Mark Wilson/Getty Images; pp. 38 © AP Images; p. 41 Photo courtesy of Lockheed Martin. © 2012 All Rights Reserved; p. 44 Sgt. Daniel Love; p. 52 U.S. Navy/Getty Images; interior graphics: © iStockphoto.com/P_Wei (camouflage), © iStockphoto.com/Oleg Zabielin (silhouette), © iStockphoto.com/gary milner (texture).

Designer: Brian Garvey; Editor: Nicholas Croce; Photo Researcher: Marty Levick